Bea's Niece

by
David Gow

Playwrights Canada Press
Toronto Canada

Bea's Niece © Copyright 1997 David Gow
Playwrights Canada Press
54 Wolseley St., 2nd fl. Toronto, Ontario CANADA M5T 1A5
Tel: (416) 703-0201 Fax: (416) 703-0059
e-mail: orders@puc.ca   http://www.puc.ca

Playwrights Canada Press acknowledges the support of The Canada
Council for the Arts for our publishing programme
and the Ontario Arts Council.

Cover design: Jodi Armstrong
Cover photo: David Gow
Image Manipulation: Mark Schoenberg

Canadian Cataloguing in Publication Data
David Gow, 1964-
        Bea's Niece

A play

ISBN 0-88754-489-0

I. Title.

PS8563.0877B42 2000   C812'.54   C99-933118-3
PR9199.3.G68B42 2000

First edition: March 2000
Printed and bound by Hignell Printing at Winnipeg, Manitoba, Canada.

ACKNOWLEDGEMENTS

I would like to thank everyone who has assisted me in the development of the play. See also pages two and three. I would also like to thank the following individuals, organizations and their staffs for their assistance and support in bringing this play to the public:

25th St. Theatre Centre, American Jewish Theatre Association, City of Saskatoon, Canada Council For The Arts, Canadian Stage Company, Dramatists Guild, Inc., Factory Theatre, Fallis Management, Ontario Arts Council, Playwrights Union of Canada, Playwrights Canada Press, Sarasota Jewish Commiunity Centre Florida, Saskatchewan Arts Board, Reisler Talent, Theatre Communications Group, Toronto Arts Council, Volcano Theatre (Canada), York University Department Of Theatre, York University Department of Psychology.

David Abel, Don Adams, David Baile, The Baugniet Family, Lisa Bayliss, Martha Blum, Martin Bragg, Dave Carley, Jonny Cuthbert, Joseph Drapell and family,

Prof. Norman S. Endler, Prof. Gordon L. Flett, Ken Gass, Peter Gianakos, Rebbe Gottfried (Jerusalem) Prof. Robert Fothergill, Harry Broughton Gow & The Gow Family, The Gow-Cooper Family, Michael Healey, Josh & Anne Heilman, Rob Von Herrman, Iamage Manipulation, Rachel Katz, Rabbi Kay (Jerusalem), Tom Kerr, The Kalo Family, Ron Lea & Anne-Lie Des Aulniers, Michael A. Levine, Paul Lampert, Glyniss Leyshon, Ross Manson, Hrothgar Mathews & Family, Sean Mc Cann, Hamish Mc Ewan, Charles Northcote, Michael Petrasek, Jacob Potashnik,Thom Richardson, Angela Rebeiro, Prof. Judith Rudakoff, Rabbi Rock (Jerusalem), Richard Rose, Vittorio Rossi, Prof. David Rotenberg, Prof. Don Rubin, Dr. Raymond Rupert, Howard Rypp & Family, Mark Schoenberg, Rabbi Paul Sheldon, Amela Simich, Patricia Talbot, Sally Szuster, Rabbi Shlomo Rock (Jerusalem), Vivian Palin, Dean Phil Silver, Prof. Ron Singer, Brian Quirt, Colleen Wagner, Carrie Zdunich. All of my teachers past, present and future.

NOTES ON PUNCTUATION

In this script, ".." indicates the character is looking for words or has run out of words; "..." indicates a thought before a line or a thought that continues after the line. "-" between words indicates compression, or a continuous breath. ";" indicates a progression of thought, a silent therefore, which takes slightly more time than one would allow a comma – without making two sentences seperate thoughts of the sentence. "," indicates a brief rest, a breath. Full caps indicate importance, intensity and occasionally shouting.

Born in 1964, David grew up in the Ottawa area and Montréal, studied at Glebe Collegiate and Concordia University. He wrote and acted regularly while still a teenager, performed character monologues in stand-up clubs, and read political commentary in bars, years before he could buy a drink. In 1992, Joe's Theatre, a Toronto company, produced David's first full-length play. In 1993, David was invited to join the Chalmers Playwrights Unit at Tarragon. His second full-length play was produced by Montreal's Centaur Theatre. More recently *Cherry Docs*, which premiered with Volcano and Factory Theatre, has seen productions across Canada, is part of the repertoire of Nephesh Theatre, Israel, and makes its American premiere at the Wilma Theatre in Philadelphia. David has an M.F.A. in Playwriting and Theatre from York University. His most recent play, *Bea's Niece*, has just premiered at The 25th Street Theatre in Saskatoon. David has adapted his work for radio and film.

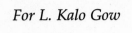
For L. Kalo Gow

FOREWORD

By Glen Cairns

"Art is not truth. Art is a lie which allows us to approach the truth."-Pablo Picasso

When David Gow first sent me a copy of his new play, I was intrigued by the complexity and ingenuity of its structure, and then I fell in love with the characters. When some people talk about writing in a non-linear style, it often means they don't know how to tell a story—David does. The play is the simple story of Anne Hirsch—a crazy lady who gets better—which has been constructed in the style of a cubist painting: a single object portrayed simultaneously from many different points of view. Like the Picasso painting of a woman who has her nose stuck on the wrong side of her face and her eyes pointing in different directions, with the shadow of her nose falling in the opposite direction to the source of light, revealing many different facets of her personality in a single portrait. This style of work challenges our preconceived notions about the person or object in the portrait. And that is what we have attempted to do with our production—examine the inner workings of a woman who is struggling through a serious mental illness, by illuminating her from different points of view. The play is meant to be a puzzle—I hope you enjoy putting the pieces together as much as we have.

Glen Cairns
Artistic Director
25th St. Theatre
Saskatoon, Saskatchewan

CHARACTERS
(Four actors playing five characters)

ANNE HIRSCH	A novelist in her fifties.
AUNT BEA	ANNE's maternal aunt, in her seventies.
PAULA STERN	A professor of Theology and a Rabbi. Doubled by the same actress as BEA.
DR. BETH OTTIS	A psychiatrist, mid-thirties, pregnant.
BILL HIRSCH	ANNE's husband, in his fifties.

SET

Scene changes are continuous. Between some scenes a brief blackout may be effective; provided necessarily continuous dialogue is not interrupted. For example Act Two, Scene Two and Act Two, Scene Three should not be broken. A bed is at the centre of the stage. At pre-show, ten rectangular screens almost cover the width of the backstage wall. These should be curtains on tracks reminiscent of hospital privacy drapes, or alternatively, flats in tracks. These drapes or screens should be moved by the actors, except for the actor playing ANNE.

The screens are treated with paint or possibly projections as follows:
On the top third we see sky and clouds, possibly pieces of buildings which are part of a downtown skyline.
On the middle third we see a lush canopy of trees and leaves.
On the bottom third we see the fragmented specifics of particular places, ie. hospital, home, etc.

David Gow began *Bea's Niece* as part of his Graduate work with the Theatre Department at York University in 1997. The company was:

ANNE HIRSCH	Darlene Spencer & Kirsten Van Ritzen
AUNT BEA, PAULA STERN	Louise Picket
DR. BETH OTTIS	L. Kalo Gow
BILL HIRSCH	Finn White
Director & Dramaturg	Ian Ferguson

Next the play advanced with two separate in house readings at The Canadian Stage Company with the following companies:

ANNE HIRSCH	Nancy Beattie
AUNT BEA, PAULA STERN	Charmion King
DR. BETH OTTIS	Kate Trotter
BILL HIRSCH	Peter Mc Neil
Director	Katherine Kaszas
Dramaturg	Iris Turcott

ANNE HIRSCH	Dianne D'Aquila
AUNT BEA, PAULA STERN	Charmion King
DR. BETH OTTIS	Kelly Fox
BILL HIRSCH	Richard MacMillan
Director	Josie Le Grice
Dramaturg	Iris Turcott

David was playwright in residence at Factory Theatre in 1998/1999 where he continued to work on *Bea's Niece* as well as other projects. The play was read for the first time publicly, in Canada, in October 1999 at Factory Theatre as part of "Works" with the following company:

ANNE HIRSCH	Tanja Jacobs
AUNT BEA, PAULA STERN	Joyce Campion
DR. BETH OTTIS	Soo Garay
BILL HIRSCH	Larry Yachimec
Director	Josie Le Grice

Bea's Niece premiered with 25th St. Theatre of Saskatoon, Saskatchewan on November 28th, 1999.

ANNE HIRSCH	Wenna Shaw
AUNT BEA, PAULA STERN	Judith Hilderman & Rosy Frier-Dryden*
DR. BETH OTTIS	Cynthia Dyck
BILL HIRSCH	Rod MacIntyre
Director	Glenn Cairns
Dramaturgy	Iris Turcott & Glenn Cairns
Asst. To The Director	Ceara Bogan
Set & Costume Design	Jean-Marie Michaud
Lighting Design	Mark von Eschen
Stage Manager	Jim Arthur
Technical Director	Greg Roberts
Publicist	Lenore Swystun

*The role of Paula Stern was played by a second actor in this production, (rather than doubling it as was originally intended) due to a particularly aggressive flu.

ACT ONE
Scene One

Nine screens house right, one screen house left. The screen which is house right shows us some particulars of ANNE's home. On the panel, we see numerous open pill containers. ANNE is pretending to shoot the windows out of her house with an imaginary shotgun.

ANNE   *(Quietly makes the sound of a shotgun.)*

As the lights dim, we hear the sound of glass breaking, perhaps one very large piece.

ACT ONE
Scene Two

Eight screens house right, two screens house left. A private room in a psychiatric hospital is referenced in the second screen house left.

ANNE   *(In bed. Speaking in her sleep.)* Here's what she told me, Bea. *(Still asleep, imitating her AUNT BEA.)* There are a few things you need in order to be taken as a lady in society, dear...

AUNT BEA appears stage left, in a sharp spot, and takes over the speech.

BEA   You need a decent home, there's no question of that. You need to have somewhere to entertain. You need to have a handsome ottoman, a comfy chair or two. Decor, yes that will help. You need to have a strong sense of yourself for when you encounter difficult people. You will need to have a nice set of dishes, for example Willow-ware. People won't feel at all uncomfortable with that, but still, it's a standard. *(Short pause.)* In a sideboard's drawer, and this you need more than anything else, dearie.. Can you guess? No? Well I'll tell you. Just for herself, not guests. A lady needs a very full bottle, say twenty-six ounces, of Scotch whiskey on hand at all times. That is paramount dearie. You'll also need to have a clean, well-oiled forty-five calibre revolver, that's very important for a lady especially if your husband has a tendency to wander. *(Short pause.)* Now if you're lucky, if you want to spoil yourself, but only occasionally and only if the nerves are at their very worst. I've told you about the family's nerves and why? That's right, petty nobility, in England dear, good for you. For the nerves, but only on special occasions dearie, you will want to have a stainless steel syringe and just the tiniest supply of opium. Those last three things: scotch, a gun and some opium are the three things you need most to be a lady in any cir-cumstance.

ANNE   *(Still asleep.)* That's what she told me. That's what she told me.. she told me.

> BETH *is visibly pregnant, end of first trimester.*

BETH   *(Clapping her hands hard near ANNE's face.)* WAKE UP, C'MON ANNE FOR GOD'S SAKE WAKE UP...

ANNE   What?

BETH   WAKE UP DAMNIT.

ANNE   *(Quietly at first.)* ...Don't tell me I'm on the other side.. that I've travelled to another realm, only to be plagued by you?

BETH   I almost LOST YOU. We vacuumed enough pills out of your stomach to kill a moose. You're lucky not to be in the morgue right now, you're lucky to have a.. a.. a..

ANNE   *(Looking straight out to the audience.)* Bea. Beatrice. My maternal Aunt Bea. She was a...

BETH   ..Stop it.

ANNE   What?

BETH   TALK TO ME.

ANNE   She was a lady. She was a tea-society lady. She was a hurly-burly, hell in your face, boiling pot of water, broad..

BETH   KEEP TALKING, yes.. Now, who were you talking to?

ANNE   My audience. The audience, you see?

BETH   A window.

ANNE   My reading public, myself, that's who I was talking to.

BETH   Can I get you a pen and some paper?

ANNE   NOT ON YOUR LIFE! You think you can trick me. Ha! It's not going to happen in your lifetime, sweetie.

BETH   You don't miss your audience?

ANNE   NO. And they won't miss me. They just think they will. Let them find another authoress. I'm tired of them. I'm tired of the mail pouring through the slot in my front door like a gallon bucket full of water. And I'm tired of picking it up, and Bill's not there to to... *(Suddenly she is silent.)*

BETH   *(A short pause.)* ..People do want the best for you, but you're going to have to...

ANNE   They want the best for themselves. They'll die if they have to, just to get away, just to escape...

BETH   Yes, when someone is sick, sometimes they die.

ANNE   So why haven't I died? I've certainly tried hard enough. I didn't eat for weeks. Scarcely lost a pound.

BETH   YOU'RE NOT SICK. *(Pause.)* You must have eaten something?

ANNE   Ginger snaps. *(Pause.)* Eight every day with hot water.

BETH   And?

ANNE   Hot water.

BETH   And sleeping pills.. Half a medicine chest.. God knows what all. That's quite a diet. *(Pause.)* It's a miracle you're still alive.

ANNE   It's a fabulous diet. And you don't lose a pound ..My reading public.

BETH   You see them, do you?

ANNE   Oh yes. A very troubled lot. Why don't you go see *them* shrinko?

BETH   Don't call me shrinko. They're not trying to OFF THEMSELVES.

ANNE   Sorry, honey. But you are a shrink. You mustn't shrink from that. No shirking being a shrink.

BETH   I'd like to hear if you had any dreams.

ANNE   NOW?

BETH   Yes.

ANNE   You know very well what I dream.

BETH   Tell me about one.

ANNE   You tell me. Tell me what I dream about. I don't want you mixing me up with some dollar nine-ty-nine fruitcake down the ward.

BETH   I know very well who you are. I'm your biggest living fan; I'm an admirer as well as your physician.

ANNE   C'mon, tell me.

BETH   You dream that you are God.

ANNE   Correction.

BETH   What?

ANNE   I know that I am God.

BETH   Oh no..

ANNE   WHILST DREAMING, yes, I know that I am God.

BETH   Omnipotence. A desire for..

ANNE   Who's without it, sweetheart? Didn't you get just a little tuck on your tummy last year?

BETH   A tuck on my tummy..? What are you talking about?

ANNE   God.

BETH   Yes, you dream you're God.. a marked desire for omnipotence.. it's NOT OKAY to hurt yourself. I could lose my license.

ANNE   ..It could be just a good dream.

BETH   Your childish-three-year-old-Id is trying to...

ANNE   Yes, the little girl, the three-year-old me. The one who wants to be told she's right, and pretty, and smart, and blameless. The one who has done no wrong in the world. Who was careful to eat her peas properly. Who was given the family Willow-ware to eat off at age three because she was so good.

BETH   Do you remember being three?

ANNE   Yes. Perfectly clearly. Doesn't everyone?

BETH   No. Not everyone.

ANNE   My whatsit has come out at this late stage in my life for a walk, because she's tired of hiding away. She's tired of living only in a photograph on the bureau.

BETH   You're sure you don't want a pen and paper?

ANNE   NO.

BETH   YOU'RE NOT DONE. You're simply not. No one's ever DONE, even when whatever you're chasing after seems to get away; out of sight, out of reach you've got to...

ANNE   Is it really so impossible to have even a small sherry here? It's five o'clock and Bill used to every day... bring me just the smallest of sherries.

BETH   NO. They just this morning had to put a pump... Maybe when you get well enough to go home, you can go back to that.

ANNE   I'm not going home.

BETH   Well in a few days, you come to my office, you might have one.

ANNE   You can't get me to write, and you can't lure me out into the lurid world. Are you getting that?

BETH   *(Pause.)* Some patients who come to me actually want to get well, it's a tangible goal for them.

ANNE   How many times have I asked you for something? Something to take the edge off. To get my mind just a little bit away from me.

BETH   We've tried that...

ANNE   We didn't try enough. There has to be something, there has to be something that's *good for me.*

BETH   ...What happened?

ANNE   They say, I ran amuck.

BETH   Who says?

ANNE   You know who, I am not paranoiac. The staff, the staff at the bookstore. I think we should try again.

BETH   This is beyond the bookstore.. We've tried a number of mood elevators.

ANNE   Try a mood escalator, ejaculator, ejector. *(Short pause.)* Hector me, sideways if necessary, out of this state.

BETH   It would simply heighten your depression, intensify it, we can't afford that, particularly now after this...

ANNE   RIGHT.

BETH   This is because you have a very big mind, a very large imagination. Once you allow yourself a little disorder, it's as though.. I don't know.. It's like..

ANNE   ..It's like trying to dust the Banff Springs Hotel with a Q-tip.

BETH   Yes that's an apt image. It's...

ANNE   It's what?

BETH   It's frankly a little exhausting.

ANNE   Let's take a break, put me on some whatchamacallits.

BETH   NOT AN OPTION.

ANNE   ..I wrote those books, and I can tear them up if I like.

BETH   The, perhaps defiantly backward, perspective of the staff is that the books are the property of the publisher.

ANNE   God, it was satisfying. Standing there in the aisle tearing up those novels. The first two particularly, do you have any idea what they cost me to write?

BETH   I have a sense of it.

ANNE   Quintuple it. That's how hard it was. Just pulling them apart like that, ripping them, and ripping.. Oh, I think on it as perhaps one of the most lucid, most enjoyable moments of my entire career. Better than most of the prizes and awards.

BETH   ..Better than *income*?

ANNE   *(Rising volume.)* Much better. Much more satisfying. You can only do so much with money. It can't bring someone back from the dead, not yet anyway.

BETH   You definitely don't need more mood elevators.

ANNE   That's your orthodoxy, your God. If you want me better, find out what the hell is wrong with me. Start there.

BETH   That's what everyone wants to know.. *(Pause.)* I've got more colleagues looking over my shoulder than if I'd found an invisible man.

ANNE   Well I'm glad we're causing a splash. See if they'll shut down an expressway for me.

BETH   Yes we are. You do want to get better don't you?

ANNE   What's better than this?

BETH   NOT HAVING YOUR STOMACH PUMPED
OUT. Functioning, interacting, even seeking
fun... pleasure.

ANNE   Have you been reading the personals again?

BETH   Functioning would be better. You'd feel better if
you got back to writing. *(A silence.)* Think about
it.

ANNE   You want to cram my mind back into my head.
That's why I call you *shrinko*. You want to
shrink down my mind to a manageable size
again.

BETH   Yes, but you're enjoying the suffering far too
much to co-operate. You're headed straight for
cotton-candy, victim land, a big sticky, libidi-
nized black death. You can forget it, I AM NOT
GOING TO LET YOU..

ANNE   *(Short pause.)* I don't enjoy it; it's simply there.
My mind has moved into a new realm of fic-
tion.

BETH   Yes? Please, tell me about it.

ANNE   Fiction which exists only in my head, understand? It's like wall-to-wall fiction.

BETH   I see, virtual fiction. *(Pause.)* No need to write it
out huh?

ANNE   Yes. Eighteen hours a day. Zip, zip, zip. The
only rest is sleep.

BETH   Well, turn the volume down. Turn off the
switch.

ANNE You seem to not want me dead, all these hero-
ics.. That's the only way I could turn off the
switch. That would be peace and quiet.

BETH: No, you can do it by yourself... pills, death, it's
all an escape.

ANNE I CAN'T. Where the hell is Bill? I'm sick now,
where the hell is he?

BETH You know where.

ANNE He could come for a visit at least.

BETH No, he can't.

ANNE At least in my head he could, he could come
and talk on my stratosphere-o-net.

BETH You can remember him. You can imagine what
he might say.

ANNE No, I can bring him here for hours at a stretch.
This is meta-reality. But still, he won't stay, not
long enough for me to.. I want Bill.

BETH He's gone.

ANNE GET HIM IN HERE.

BETH ..He's dead.

    *A silence, then starting very quietly and
    rising in volume.*

ANNE I've begged you not to say that. I have begged
you again and again. Why must you say that
word? It's not a good word at all. YOU
SHOULD HAVE YOUR MOUTH WASHED
OUT WITH SOAP.

BETH   Don't talk to me... Don't talk to me like I'm a little.. I'm a FULLY GROWN WOMAN and a Doctor!

> *ANNE bursts out laughing. BETH exits, part way and comes back in.*

BETH   I need a break, I'm going to go... look at your blood.

> *Again, BETH leaves part way, she is stopped by ANNE's request.*

ANNE   Don't you go yet.. please.

BETH   You're going to have to try harder.

ANNE   I do, I do try.

BETH   Keep trying.

ANNE   I will sweetie, I promise, where's Bill?

BETH   I'M NOT YOUR..

> *BILL enters. He is in his late fifties, a nice-looking man. He is carrying a cardboard box.*

BETH   I need a couple of minutes to myself. *(BETH exits.)*

ACT ONE
Scene Three

*Seven screens house right, three screens
house left. We are still in the hospital.*

ANNE   Bill... are you?

BILL   I'm not..

ANNE   I know. Let's pretend though, can we pretend
you are?

BILL   Yeah.

ANNE   Do I look nice, sweetie? My skin, my hair?

BILL   You look radiant, let me give you a kiss. *(He
kisses her passionately)*

ANNE   You're too kind. I look a mess. *(ANNE gets up
out of bed)* Here you take the bed, you're the
one who isn't well. You put your feet up.

BILL   Thanks, I'll have to take off my shoes.

ANNE   Don't worry, they change the sheets constantly.
It makes them feel calm–in control of some-
thing.

BILL   I brought you your siddur, some Sabbath candles, your menorah, a mezuzah *(He takes these
articles of religious observance out of the box.[a siddur is a prayer book. The Sabbath candles are three
short, plain, white candles, the menorah is plain
brass, with seven stems, and its own smaller candles
in a box.] BILL places these articles on top of
ANNE's chest of drawers, where they must remain
visible for the duration of the play. As BILL turns
around rubbing his hands, he's handling some
magicians "flash paper", which creates a bright*

*flame momentarily in the palms of his hands.
ANNE might not see the flame but the audience
must.)* What can I do for you?

ANNE   I know we've been over some of this a hundred
times before, but there's always a few things I
have to ask you. Do you mind?

BILL   Go on.

ANNE   What do I do with pennies, again?

BILL   I've told you...

ANNE   Tell me again.

BILL   You count them out at the counter, when you're
in a line-up that isn't too long. When there's no
one behind you.

ANNE   I used to wonder what the hell you bothered
for. Then afterwards, once you were gone. I
noticed pennies and change piling up in my
purse. Copper and nickel and silver all over the
house, mixed with dust.

BILL   It gets very messy. Things can get messy if you
don't take care of them.

ANNE   Can I tell you what I've done?

BILL   Sure.

ANNE   I have a mason jar for each of the coins. I fill
them up to the top.

BILL   Then?

ANNE   Then I, I'm not sure what. Oh yes, I know now.
The pennies I give to someone on the street.
The other coins. I put them in my pockets and
pay for coffee, or taxi fare, subway fare.

BILL   Good for you.

ANNE   It never occurred to me, while you were
around. 'What happens to my change?' I never
thought much of it.

BILL   And your purse would get heavier and heavier.

ANNE   Did you mind doing it?

BILL   Well...

ANNE   Did you?

BILL   You needed a lot of taking care of.

ANNE   And you took care of me.

BILL   It was a lot of work.

ANNE   But we never really had money problems...

BILL   The early years. After you quit social work. A
steady diet of rice, lentils and hope.

ANNE   Did you mind?

BILL   Yes I did mind. I would mind when you would
tell me to hurry up in a store to stop being so
fussy with the change.

ANNE   That's a little thing, though.

BILL   Part of the larger problem. Are you trying?

ANNE   Trying what?

BILL   Are you trying to get better, dear?

ANNE   I don't see the use. You're not here. If you were
here, really here. I could be better like that.
(*Snaps her fingers.*) Without you it seems fruit-
less.

BILL   You have to do it for yourself. Be selfish, it was never a problem before.

ANNE   *(Pause.)* That hurt.

BILL   True.

ANNE   I wrote for you. You were my favourite reader. My only true reader. You knew where everything came from. All the secrets. You saw the knitting needles at work. No one else ever has.

BILL   Such needles. You have to write for yourself.

ANNE   I don't need the amusement. I have contempt...

BILL   Why?

ANNE   You know why. The last book. A woman's husband is ill, she doesn't have time to notice because she's so involved with her career as a painter...

BILL   And the husband gets more ill, and more...

ANNE   Yes. I started the book a year before you got ill. I think it made you ill.

BILL   That's not entirely true.

ANNE   Entirely?

BILL   You can't make me ill now.

ANNE   No, and I can't bring you back. I could write twelve books in which a husband comes back from the dead and I don't think you would.

BILL   Most probably right.

ANNE   ..Did you have to die?

BILL   I think so. They did everything they could.

ANNE   (*A pause.*) They keep moving the subway stops around. Mostly I take cabs because of it.

BILL   (*Teasing.*) They don't move the subway stops.

ANNE   That's how it feels. I get on the subway, I aim for a familiar stop—and before I know it, the train's at the end of the line. There's a nuclear reactor out there, you know? I think a person's got to be careful in that end of town.

BILL   You have to pay attention.

ANNE   Yes, that's what it is. The stops don't really move do they?

BILL   No.

ANNE   When do I vacuum?

BILL   You know.

ANNE   Tell me.

BILL   Vacuum on Saturday mornings, before anything else.

ANNE   What if I were to write?

BILL   It could wait.

ANNE   And the groceries?

BILL   Always after the vacuuming.

ANNE   Okay, I'll do it your way. If I get better it will be your way.

BILL   You only have to please yourself now, Annie.

ANNE   Do you know how many hours there are in a day without you?

BILL   Tell me.

ANNE   Twenty-four-thousand.

BILL   Really?

ANNE   Yes. And do you know what the sun does every morning without you?

BILL   Rises?

ANNE   Full of belligerence, each and every day. Sickening really.

BILL   How about the moon?

ANNE   It longs for you. The moon misses you, and it tells me so by giving me an aching in my gut.

BILL   You haven't lost your platinum sense of humour, Annie.

ANNE   I misplaced it for a while. It was stuck under the fridge for a year-and-a-half.

BILL   Not really?

ANNE   Ask anyone. They said I was dead. They still do.

BILL   Do you have to be so grand about it?

ANNE   Am I?

BILL   I don't know, maybe not.

ANNE   We had a good life, didn't we?

BILL   Don't make me lie.
ANNE   It was mostly good, wasn't it?

BILL   Lie.

ANNE   It was... it was a life wasn't it?

BILL   At times.

ANNE   You're hard on me. Harder all the time.
Remember when we had the kitchen floor re-
done. We made love on the cool tiles. My bottom cool, the rest of me all warm.

BILL   That was nice.

ANNE   The months we spent in the country every
year?

BILL   It wasn't all bad.

ANNE   I'd like to think you have some good memories.

BILL   Don't quiz me too much then.

ANNE   All right. What do I do with pennies?

BILL   Put them in a jar.

ACT ONE
Scene Four

The hospital room. Six screens house right,
four screens house left. Amongst the
screens, fragments of a streetscape, promi-
nent, the inside of a convenience store.

BEA   ...It was what you'd call a long drive.

ANNE   You came just for me?

BEA   I heard you weren't well...

ANNE   What did you hear?

BEA   What I heard, and what I know are two different things.

ANNE   You heard that I went off my rocker...

BEA   I *know* that you will be all right, I know that
you are suffering from the family dilemma. You
remember what I told you when you were
younger...

ANNE   Yes, about the family's nerves...

BEA   Yes. And how you've got them. God knows I've
had them on and off most of my life.

ANNE   What can I do about it?

BEA   It will pass eventually, it's largely a question of
time.

ANNE   How long did it take you to get here?

BEA   I think it was about a week, I don't count every
day anymore, it spoils the fun.

ANNE   You drove all the way from the top of the Rockies?

BEA   From the brim of the Pacific Ocean dear; stop worrying about it, I can't fly, I don't believe we were meant to.

ANNE   By yourself?

BEA   No, no. I have a gentleman friend who wanted to come east, he helped with the driving and he's handy for a couple of other things as well. We stopped along the way and had a bit of a bender here and there. Apparently you can't drink while you're driving anymore, but you can still drive the next day.

ANNE   What did you come for?

BEA   I wanted to help you sort yourself out dear, it's not nice for a lady to be alone with the nerves, you need someone to take an interest. Someone who understands.

ANNE   Thank you for coming, auntie.

BEA   It was nothing, I wouldn't have come if I hadn't felt like it.

ANNE   How much time, will it take?

BEA   Quite a lot, unless you suddenly get hold of yourself. That happened to me a couple of times. I woke up all better, signed the forms and left by noon the next day.

ANNE   I've been seeing a psychiatrist for a year or more, I never dreamt I'd need one.

BEA   I've been seeing psychologists, psychiatrists, ministers, priests and rabbis, concerned family and nosy neighbours since I was fifteen. They are.. very well meaning. What else have you tried?

ANNE   I've tried sleeping for days...

BEA   That can work sometimes.

ANNE   I've tried not eating.

BEA   That can't hurt, too much.

ANNE   I tried medication.

BEA   Bit of a ride that, isn't it?

ANNE   That's about all. What else is there?

BEA   There's plenty more under God's bright heavens; as well as a few things you might find elsewhere. Have you tried having a man, for a while?

ANNE   Yes, there's Martin, he's a friend mostly.

BEA   Men can be very diverting, all their little problems and worries. They can keep your lap warm, or even occasionally make it hot, that can help.

ANNE   It has helped to have his love.

BEA   Yes, but obviously, it hasn't done the full job. Have you tried a drinking cure?

ANNE   A drinking cure? Honestly, Auntie. I wouldn't know where to begin.

BEA   There must be some place you can go to get rip roaring drunk, for a few days, a week or two at a stretch?

ANNE   Not that I can think of.

BEA   Well, if it's not your habit, then it might not be best. And you have your reputation to think of, I suppose. Everyone in the world seems to

know who you are, these days. You haven't put
me in any of your little storybooks, have you
dear?

ANNE   No, never. I never wanted to.

BEA   Promise?

ANNE   Yes, promise.

(*A silence.*)

BEA   It was Bill, wasn't it?

ANNE   It wasn't *him.*

BEA   It was the fact that he. (*She stops politely.*)

ANNE   Yes.

BEA   You remember Teen Harrison who lived near
me in the sixties.

ANNE   I remember you talking about her.

BEA   She had a dachshund called Willy. Willy was a
pure bred, and had a very nice disposition. A
gentlemen of a dog, if there ever was one.
Everyone thought she should breed him, everyone wanted a dog rather like him for their own
home. Teen never had a word of disagreement
from that dog. She took him off to the kennel,
and he was presented with a very pretty little
bitch called Maggie, or some such ludicrous
name. She really was a pretty little thing,
almost blonde if you can imagine. There was
Maggie in the prime of her heat. Howling and
clawing at the floor, chewing her tail till they
had to wrap it in duct tape and cayenne pepper
to keep her from biting it off. Willy was put in
the room with her; and for most dogs the scent
of Maggie would have set them up for the job,
just as soon as they got near the building. Willy

looked at her; Teen said he looked positively worried. He just stood there looking, not knowing what to do. His poor little nose started to run. It could've been the cayenne pepper, but probably wasn't. The kennel owner couldn't believe it, he tried to encourage Willy to mount Maggie. Quite a macho type he was. Willy went into a dead faint. His knees buckled and he hit the floor like a creature shot through the head. He lost control of his bladder, and had a little wee right there on the floor; something he'd never done, even as a puppy. Teen was utterly convinced that Willy was homosexual. I never had imagined there were homosexual dogs, but I could certainly see it from that time on. When you get to know a dog, really know it as a person, it's easy enough to see. It's nice to see you laughing dearie; you've always had a voluptuous laugh. Like liquid in a ladle.

ANNE   I can't believe you never wrote, Bea.

BEA   Never had time. There's more. Years later Teen was told by a vet, that Willy was also a diabetic. So there he was in his old age, a full-fledged, insulin dependent, diabetic, gay dachshund. *(Pause.)* He wore a bow tie on his collar most of his life. Do you have the point yet, dearie?

ANNE   I'm not sure. Does there have to be a point?

BEA   Willy could not have changed any of that about himself for all the tea in China. He loved Teen dearly, but even a dog can't spend his life pretending to be something he's not.

ANNE   This relates to Bill?

BEA   He couldn't do more than he did, that's all.

ANNE   It's nice you're here, you're not arguing with me. Everyone wants to argue all the time. *(Pause.)* Men in convenience stores ask me if

I'm going to *buy* the milk. I find myself cradling two quarts of a dairy's finest as though it were the child I never had. I've been standing *here* God only knows how long. Could be an hour I suppose. Could as easily be a month.

BEA   It will pass with time. Give yourself time.

ANNE   I sometimes don't think I want it to pass.

BEA   That's the worst, don't give way to those thoughts. They are the deadliest of ideas.

ANNE   I like you so much, Auntie. You were always my favourite, and Mom wouldn't let me see you...

BEA   Your Mom had her own problems to deal with.

ANNE   Will you come and see me again?

BEA   Of course, that's what I came for. I have to go now though, I left "the handsome one" in the car, and we have to find a place to stay. I haven't got a license plate on the car and as I remember big cities, they're quite picky about just that sort of little detail.

ANNE   You will come back?

BEA   Yes.

ANNE   Are you here, are you really here?

BEA   As I live and breathe, dearie.

ANNE   Can you leave something here for me to hold onto, so that I will know you were here.

BEA   I don't see why not. I'll leave you this fresh pack of cigarettes, it's my back up pack, I'll get another. Do you remember my brand, sweetie?

ANNE   Dunhills, always Dunhills.

BEA   The tastiest there is. *(She gives the pack to ANNE.)*

ANNE   When will you come back, Auntie?

BEA   Tomorrow, ...something like that.

ANNE   Don't lose track of when.

BEA   I won't. You will get better.

ANNE   I hope so.

BEA   Bye, bye sweetie, must go.

ANNE   Don't.

BEA   Must.

ANNE   Don't, don't...

BEA   Be brave now, or Auntie won't ever come back again.

ANNE   I... Okay, I promise.

> *BEA leaves, ANNE is left cradling a pack-age of Dunhill cigarettes, rocking it like a baby. She stands still speaking to herself quietly. BETH enters. She remains at the end of the first trimester of her pregnancy.*

ANNE   Don't, don't, don't I promise I won't.
             Don't, don't, don't, I promise..

BETH   Anne?

ANNE   Don't.

BETH   Anne.

ANNE   A full-fledged, insulin dependent, diabetic, gay dachshund. He wore a bow tie on his collar most of his life.

BETH   Anne, what are you talking about?

ANNE   Oh. Hello. And why aren't you pregnant now?

BETH   ..I am. *(Short pause.)* Very much so.

ANNE   The last time I saw you, you *looked* pregnant.

BETH   Here put your hand on my stomach. *(Gesturing to her stomach.)* See.

ANNE   ..No.

BETH   Here. *(She places ANNE's hand on her stomach.)*

> *ANNE is silenced by this; she doesn't move for a moment, she is breathless.*

ANNE   *(Regaining herself.)* Not everyone wants to share in the baby, tummy touching. *(Pause.)* Not everyone wants a goat's milk enema before breakfast... Some of us just want to be left alone...

BETH   *(Overlapping.)* Ahh. Who were you talking to before?

ANNE   My Aunt Bea.

BETH   That's nice. How is she?

ANNE   She's delightful. You'll meet her.

BETH   I will, will I?

ANNE   Don't talk riddles. Yes you shall, shan't you?

BETH   Where did you get the cigarettes Anne?

·**ANNE**   Bea brought them. She drove across the country, with no license plate and a man she calls "the handsome one" entertaining her the whole way.

BETH   Am I meant to believe this as reality?

ANNE   I really don't care what you believe, she was just here a minute ago. If you touch the floor with your hands you might feel the warmth where she stood.

BETH   Might I?

ANNE   Yes you might. Stop being so god damn clinical. She was here, bring in a forensic unit if you need to. You'll find shafts of her hair. You'll find particles of her skin in the dust on the jade plant. Her scent is still in the air...

BETH   Easy now.

ANNE   ...Her scent, a mix of talcum powder liberally applied, cut through by tiny, nervously sucked triangular Vicks cough drops. She glanced out the window, toward her now unlicensed car, parked in the tow zone.

BETH: I think you need to be getting this down.

ANNE: YOU GET IT DOWN. You're not believing a word I'm saying.

BETH: Let's sit you down, you talk, I'll listen and we'll sort it out together.

ANNE: Go to hell.

BETH: I'm going to sit down, why don't we sit?

                    ANNE calms herself sitting on the bed,
                    rocking back and forth a little.

BETH   I was worried okay? This is not the neighbourhood to go for a stroll in, dressed in a bathrobe.

ANNE   I didn't go anywhere.

BETH   Tell me about your aunt.

ANNE   She drove here from the Coast, it took her a
week or more...

BETH   And this is not a story?

ANNE   Look at these cigarettes. These are real, she
gave them to me.

BETH   Good, okay.

ANNE   This is her brand.

BETH   How old is she?

ANNE   Plenty old, that's not a very polite question, is
it? She's a lady, she's, all right she's in her sev-
enties let's say.

BETH   ...Your Aunt Bea, whom I have seen you have a
number of imaginary conversations with, has
driven across the country in a car with no
license, in order to bring you a pack of cigarettes?

ANNE   Stranger things have happened in the natural
course of history.

BETH   Yes, I'll grant you that.

ANNE   I don't need it granted...

BETH   I believe it's within the realm of the possible...

ANNE   Smart ass. You're talking to me as though I
were some kind of idiot.

BETH   I'm just trying to sort things out.

ANNE   Bea, is coming back, I promised to be brave, and to be a good girl, and she said she'd come back...

BETH   ..Yes, she undoubtedly will.

ANNE   *(Going on a bit of a tear.)* Get a police dog in here; did you know that a dog can tell fifty different physical facts about another dog just by a scent? The scent left in urine. Get a human to do that and they might not die at the wrong time. Dogs can track a human in a forest or through an underground mall by the minuscule DNA print which lives in scent; even though it may well have been transferred, only through the sole of a shoe.

BETH   Okay, Anne, okay.

ANNE   And, in case you didn't know it, there's also a drinking cure for what I have.

BETH   Do you really think a seventy-something year old woman came across the country..?

ANNE   Yes, YES, is it so stupid? Is it so HARD TO BELIEVE for even a minute?

BETH   I'd like to believe it, I really would.

ANNE   So why don't you?

BETH   *(Pause.)* Because, they came and got me.

ANNE   Who did?

BETH   The orderlies.

ANNE   When?

BETH   Twenty minutes ago.

ANNE Then what happened?

BETH They brought me to a store a block and a half from here.

ANNE Yes.

BETH The owner said you had taken some cigarettes, and that you were rocking them in your arms as though you were holding a baby. That you were talking to yourself.

ANNE I don't think that's possible.

BETH I saw it. I was there.

ANNE I am... uh... I am a little ...I find this very confusing.

BETH I want to help you sort it out.

ANNE Yes, we have to try, to sort some of this out.

BETH ..I've been trying to..

ANNE And get me some Vicks cough drops too, please.

BETH No problem.

ANNE To show you, to show you I'm thinking straight, I'm not even going to ask for Bill. Bill can't pretend any more than can a dog.

BETH Right.

ANNE ...Straighten things out.

BETH Let's put you to bed.
ANNE I'm very tired. It's been a busy day.

BETH Yes.

ANNE   I've had a lot of visitors.

BETH   Shh, that's right, shhh.

ANNE   Goodnight.

BETH   Goodnight.

ANNE   I'll be good, I promise.

BETH   It's all right. Shh. *(Pause.)* Goodnight, Mom. *(Short pause.)* Where did that come from?

ACT ONE
Scene Five.

Five screens house right, five screens house left. The fifth screen, house left, clearly references the hospital again. BILL enters with a large box, ANNE wakes as he begins unloading the box.

BILL   *(Quietly.)* Morning, Annie.

ANNE   Bill.

BILL   Hello. *(Pause.)* I brought a few things for you.

ANNE   ...That's nice of you.

BILL   Your portable. *(He unpacks a typewriter.)* Five hundred sheets of Weyerhauser, some white out; the doctors said, this was a good idea.

ANNE   I'm not writing.

BILL   In case... in case you feel like it, you know I don't mind either way. Also, your cough drops... *(He unpacks four packets of Vicks.)*

ANNE   ...*My* cough drops?

BILL   Yes, Anne. Seven packs a week for the last ten years, since you threw out the Dunhills. Don't make me remember everything, I'm tired too. *(He unpacks some talcum powder.)* Your baby powder... now I have got to...

ANNE   I use baby powder and cough drops?

BILL   Annie, don't... I have got to get to the license bureau, before there's a line up, or I will lose the whole day.

ANNE   ...Why?

BILL   The license has to be renewed on the car.
       Someone has to look after these things...

ANNE   Bill, I'm so mixed up... you have no idea.

BILL   I know, sweetheart.

ANNE   I had a... I thought you were dead, that you had
       died of a disease, and I had ignored it until it
       was too late.

BILL   (*A little uneasily.*) I've always tried to be accom-
       modating, but... really dear. I can't die till my
       time comes. Not even to support a fantasy, not
       even, given the alleviation it might bring.

ANNE: I don't want you to die, honestly.

BILL: Well, there's a spot of luck, because I'm not
       going to. I am going to go to the license bureau,
       and then I will do some grocery shopping...

ANNE   (*Holding back a wave of emotion.*) Bill, please,
       please don't tease. Don't tease me now.

BILL   Anne, I can't stay to talk; the Doctors say, in
       some way, I may be upsetting you.

ANNE   You're not ill...

BILL   *You're* ill, I'm not even feverish. I've got to
       get...

ANNE   Stay, please stay a few moments, until I know
       what's real.

BILL   Annie, you promised me. You promised and
       promised. You said: "I won't."

ANNE   What did I promise?

BILL	I can't do this; I can't *think for* you. It's work enough, to think for oneself. There's only so much room in my head.
ANNE	Bill, I want so much to come home... I really, really want out of here. If only you would...
BILL	*(Tensing.)* That's, what you promised. That you would stay at least one week, that you wouldn't make me take you home again. Annie, I must, must, leave.
ANNE	If you do, I may never get my mind back. I don't know what you're talking about.. The cough drops, the talcum powder, the license...
BILL	I just wanted to make sure you had your basics, you need to hold onto a habit or two, even here.
ANNE	You didn't die?
BILL	*(Trying to be reasonable.)* Annie, who would take care of your change, if I, died?
ANNE	I'd put it in Mason jars.
BILL	*(Laughing.)* That's good. *(Pause.)* Do you not want these things, the.. bric-a-brac that I brought you?
ANNE	It belongs to Aunt Bea, even the license bureau...
BILL	Your Aunt Bea? It's been a while since we heard from her.
ANNE	Never mind, you're here.
BILL	*(Deliberately.)* But I can't stay.
ANNE	*(Desperately.)* Bill, I don't know what time is anymore. Do you understand what that means?

I've lost my place in time, I'm not entirely sure what year it is.

BILL   Entirely?

ANNE   I have an idea...

BILL   Hold onto it. *(He begins to exit, with his back to her.)* Annie, place your trust in the doctors, that's what you promised, one week.

ANNE   Bill, I am not going to make it, without you...

BILL   YES YOU ARE. *(He turns around painfully slowly, swallowing down his emotion; he speaks beginning with a whisper.)* Do you think this is easy for me? Do you think I can stand to see you like this for one second? You are my best, brightest, friend, my lover, and companion, my one and only Annie. Titan of the typewriter; and I have to tell you every moment, who you are. How do you think it feels? It's a knife in my back, sweetheart.

ANNE   One thing, just one. You've always been straight with me, you've always told the absolute truth...

BILL   ...I have been lying for years. Everyday, I have to lie a hundred times, to protect you from yourself. "No, I don't mind... No, it's okay... No, you go ahead... No, I'm not worried." My friends come over for dinner, and in the middle of a five course meal, I've prepared, with fucking pheasant no less... you get up and go to the third floor to write for fifteen hours. And in the morning, I swear you've aged yourself a year... I don't want to talk this way...

ANNE   Just tell me, are you dead?

BILL   Physically no, but inside, yes. YES, I'm dead and dying more each day... The body, the corpus. This thing here, is still with you; and some tiny part of my heart and soul. But please, leave me that much, left for myself. *(Pause.)* *Work* with the doctors, or I won't be able to come back. I can't always come back, no matter what.

ANNE Can you just tell me..?

BILL *(Again turning to leave.)* No. Didn't you hear me? Why can't you hear me? I am at the end of my rope. I am exhausted. We are none of us Gods, Annie. Not I, in any case. *(Pause.)* I can't think for you, and explain you to others, and take care of you every minute. *You* cannot seem to do it for yourself either, and that is why you are here. *(Pause.)* Tell me you'll be all right...

ANNE I don't know...

BILL LIE, FOR CHRIST'S SAKE. Lie, for me just once, woman.

ANNE *(Like granite.)* I will be fine.

BILL Thank you. I am going to the license bureau. I am going to go to a cafe and drink hot milk, till my hands stop shaking; and then I am going home to sleep for a day or two. I will be back in one week's time.

ANNE I will be; I will be; I will be fine.

BILL Good. Have a good... get better.

ANNE I will.

BILL ...Write a page or two of anything at all, you will feel better. You always do.

ANNE I said. I will.

> *BILL exits, as BETH enters, still at the end of the first trimester.*

BETH That's enough time.

BILL *(To BETH.)* I'm gone.

> *A Pause.*

ANNE I suppose you are going to tell me, just to test my poor pink and grey little brain, that you didn't, just now say to Bill, "That's enough time."

BETH I had hoped some sleep might do you some good.

ANNE Let the games begin.

BETH I said "that's enough time" to the occupational therapist who brought you the typewriter and the paper. He's a big fan of yours, I didn't want him tiring you out with questions.

ANNE That is what I'm talking about. The constant revisionism and denial that takes place here.

BETH How did you sleep?

ANNE *(Pause.)* I counted by nines to two-thousand-and sixty between eleven last night and three this morning. I'm not even sure that I should talk to you.

BETH Oh? And why not?

ANNE I don't know what time frame you exist in.

BETH Tell me what time frame you're in now.

ANNE Bill has just been here, he has had me hospitalized. I have promised to stay in hospital for one week's observation and rest. He's tired, as well.

BETH   Well that's a starting place.

ANNE   I'm glad we agree.

BETH   *(Pause.)* Now, let's place that in time.

ANNE   Good.

BETH   What is the date today?

ANNE   *(A quick tear.)* It's The Year of the Frog for all I know. *(Pause.)* In fresh water ponds, all over England brightly coloured frogs are popping up as a wink to the Bible. The Queen, carrying rugs out of Windsor Castle, after the fire, is concerned with the irregular fauna...

BETH   ...You're having me on, Anne Hirsch. You're pulling my...

ANNE   Why not? You seem to be making your own fun.

BETH   Tell me the year.

ANNE   It's... what-ever-the-hell-it-is.

BETH   *(Handing ANNE her filofax.)* Here, take a good look. Now, I did not have that made up especially, just for you. That is the actual date.

ANNE   Hooray, we've found out what day it is today. Tomorrow's therapy will include shoe-tying demonstrations.

BETH   THE TIME... the time you referred to; when you were checked in for one week's observation by your husband was three years ago, before you and I had met.

ANNE   Is that a fact?

BETH   Yes. I care for you, and would not lie.

ANNE   Don't push it, sweetie.

BETH   It is a fact.

ANNE   Don't push the, oh-so-concerned Doctor crap
on me.

BETH   Fine. Three years ago. That's when you're talking about.

ANNE   Two years, eleven months five days by your
calendar, assuming you're telling the truth.

BETH   That's a very basic assumption, without which
we cannot proceed, and without which you
will not get well.

ANNE   I'll play along.

BETH   Not good enough, YOU HAVE TO BELIEVE.

ANNE   Assuming that what occurred only minutes
ago, was in some form of reality a long time
ago, assuming that; what of it?

BETH   You got here this week. Two weeks ago, you
were in trouble at the bookstore. This week you
took too many sleeping pills. You've been here
a week, during that time you went missing for
half a day. The time you're talking about was
before your husband Bill Hirsch died from
inoperable lung cancer.

ANNE   *(Disgusted.)* You are such a liar. How many
times must I tell you not to use those words?
Dead, died, death... You're virtually obsessed...

BETH   Truth.

ANNE   You killed him. You killed him off, by entering
the room. He'll be back within one week. He
loves me, and I am his Titan.

BETH   *(Pause.)* I'm going to try something else.

ANNE   Be my guest.

BETH   Can you think of any novels where the central character is in hospital by virtue of some form of emotional incapacitation?

ANNE   Three off-hand. Can you be more specific?

BETH   Where, for example, an author is in hospital?

ANNE   *The Master and Margueritta*, by Bulgakov. Are we playing Name That Myth?

BETH   Sure.

ANNE   Could be Prometheus...

BETH   Close enough. The central character in *The Master and Margueritta* is what?

ANNE   *(Pause.)* A nut job.

BETH   Guess again.

ANNE   A writer, who suffers extravagantly.

BETH   Why?

ANNE   Any number of reasons.

BETH   Correct. But at the hub of it.

ANNE   At the hubby of it, the writer has, among other things, thrown away his manuscript, lost a lover, forsaken his art, and battles with the very devil.

BETH   And?

ANNE   ...Believes himself at one point or another to be the reincarnation of Christ, stuck in a mental hospital.

BETH   That story, transposed to our story. Who am I?

ANNE   ...The very devil.

BETH   You believe me to be the devil?

ANNE   Subconsciously I'm certain I must. Consciously, I think it, more than some small part of the time.

BETH   Right here, in my waking mind, I can tell you I believe, I know you to be a person with a very unusual gift.

ANNE   I write things down, that's all. That's the big secret, okay? I hear voices, sometimes day and night. Sometimes those voices tell me terrific stories, other times they terrify me. I am a glorified typist.

BETH   That's not true.

ANNE   Do you see it, in the corner there? The portable, the paper? That's where it takes place. A peculiar interaction between me and the page and my fingers. I've been lucky to have had it, as long as I have had it.

BETH   Let's go back to me being the devil. That's easier for me to SWALLOW, than all this false modesty crap. You love it, or you never would've done it for a minute. You make a mint from it.

ANNE   ...Yes, at times, its been my spot, just slightly inside Heaven's harsh, creaky-hinged, door. At times, its been an endless bus ride through Hell.

BETH   So, I'm the devil; or what else?

ANNE   A Doctor in a white coat?

BETH   And you know what I'm here for?

ANNE   Come on, just tell me, spit it out. You're being more circumspect than a Swiss banker.

BETH   *(Pause.)* I am going to try something radical. I want you, the conscious you, back here right now, participating in the grim reality that everyone else is sharing.

ANNE   That sounds promising.

BETH   IT'S BETTER THAN THE ALTERNATIVE. I am going to speak directly to various parts of your unconscious mind, in the hopes of reviving a modicum of conscious control. Look at me closely.

ANNE   Must I?

BETH   Yes, you must.

ANNE   I...

BETH   Must.

ANNE   Yes?

BETH   I am going to present you with a metaphor. A perhaps somewhat frightening yet scientifically accurate metaphor.

ANNE   Okay.

BETH   I stand here a woman in a white coat. I am a Doctor. Whom have I come for?

ANNE   *(Speaking in a little girl's voice.)* I don't know.

BETH   Yes, you do.

ANNE   Me? Is it me? The little girl, the three-year-old.

BETH   Yes. Stay calm.

ANNE   What do you want?

BETH   I am here to remove you.

ANNE   I'll hide away.

BETH   You mustn't.

ANNE   What will you do with me?

BETH   We must take you away.

ANNE   Where will I go?

BETH   *(A pause.)* I'm afraid you will have to die.

> *ANNE suddenly starts from where she is, breaking from the hypnotic state that she has been in. She begins pacing frantically.*

ANNE   *(In an adult voice.)* MURDERER, BLOODY MURDERER.

BETH   Remain calm, do not resist.

ANNE   MURDER, MURDER, MURDER. *(Still loudly, but not at the top of her lungs.)* She's practising bloody murder. Anne Hirsch, the well known writer is being murdered on, in Room three-o-eight, of the nut job ward.

BETH   You will not escape.

ANNE   You want to play name that song? What title tells the whole truth about a writer in a psychiatric hospital?

BETH   Irrelevant.

ANNE   Antonin Artaud, TORTURED By Psychiatrists.

BETH   WE NEED YOU BACK HERE NOW.

ANNE   Not coming.

BETH   You promised.

ANNE   THIS WOMAN HAS MURDERED EVERYONE I KNOW, everyone who comes to visit me.

BETH   There is no one else. No one else has come to visit you. There is only you and me. Can you see what I am trying to do?

ANNE   I can see you're trying bravely, very valiantly, to speak English, dear. There is no one here but you and I.

BETH   It's not you I'm fighting with...

ANNE   YOU GET THE HELL AWAY FROM ME. I will chew you up into my typewriter and rip you apart in a novel, you will be consumed by furies for centuries to come.

BETH   I'm going to sedate you. (*She reaches into a drawer and takes something out, her back to the audience.*) This is going to calm you down. (*As she turns around we see that she is loading a forty-five-calibre revolver.*)

ANNE   ...Oh Anne, she really is going to kill you.

BETH   This is a sedative, it's a mild opiate, it will put you to sleep.

ANNE   Did you say opium?

BETH   Close enough.

ANNE   Go ahead, do me.

BETH   It won't hurt a bit, be still. *(She presses the gun to ANNE's shoulder, she turns her back which masks what she is doing.)*

ANNE   Kill me, kill me now.

BETH   It may sting.

ANNE   Do it.

> *BETH turns around, she is no longer holding a gun but a syringe.*

BETH   You are going to sleep for twelve hours.

ANNE   I've seen the gun, I have the opium. Tell me Doctor, where's the scotch?

BETH   The what?

ANNE   We're back where we started. We haven't gone anywhere, how long have I been here?

BETH   A day. A month. A year.

ANNE   Who brought me here?

BETH   Go to sleep.

ANNE   I'll count to nine...

BETH   Good.

ANNE   Where's the scotch? *(ANNE falls asleep.)*

BETH: *(To herself.)* With any luck; on two fresh cubes, just plucked from the freezer, in a crystal rock's glass, on my mission-style kitchen table, the very second I walk through my front door. And there, then and there, I will lie back and have my husband crawl on top of me.. *(Pause.)* You are going to live you old bird... I throw that at you as a curse if need be.

ANNE   *(ANNE speaking in her sleep. BETH watches
ANNE.)* I am that I am. The God of the
Hebrews. I denounce the very devil in the act
of counting, which I declare to be the only
truth, which is that of time. *(Descending volume.)* One, Two, Three, Four, Five, Six, Seven.

Lights out. End of ACT ONE.

ACT TWO
Scene One
*Six screens house left, four screens house
right. ANNE is typing. We are in the hospital, but will see on the sixth screen, a ref-
erence to broken windows.*

ANNE   Five, six, seven. Five, six, seven. Six, seven...
(Covering her ears with her hands.) Ahhhhh.

BEA   Anne, some things cannot be changed for love
or money, dearie. *(Pause.)* Your father Jacob was
a great example of this. Had he not met your
Mother he would certainly have become a
Rabbi, as had his father and his father's father
etc. back 'till God knows when. Instead he married the United Church girl that my sister was.
She became a little, if I may say, overly enam-
oured with having garden tea parties; which
eventually I was thought-a little too "entertaining" to be invited to. *(Pause.)* I think I was
caught with one Minister too many. *(Short
pause.)* My, but your mother was able to keep
things polite and clean in her life. Your father
never complained; never made out for a
moment that he had made any kind of sacrifice
regarding his calling, he hadn't in his mind...
Instead he brought the *experience, intelligence*
and *wisdom* of a Rabbi to the practice of law. He
was famous for always finding an agreement
for two parties. A little unorthodox, but effective. *(Pause.)* The only time he ever came close
to failing was with me, and the man I was married to for some little years. We won't say his
name, dearie, I've not let it creep cross my lips
for years. But hubby, let's call him, after a year
of marriage to me wanted a divorce very, very
badly. I would hear nothing of it. One night I
found he had packed a small bag and put it in
his car, I knew he was fixing to leave in the
morning as though for work, and would never

come back. I stayed up most of that night thinking what to do. I helped myself to some small part of twenty-six ounces. At six thirty a.m. as the sun came up I was struck with an inspiration. I simply wouldn't let hubby go. I cut the sash cords from all of our ground floor windows with a little Swiss apple knife I kept in my handbag. The Swiss are a very inventive people, they always have been. Sash cords back in the forties were soft, nice rope, very comfortable on hubby's ankles and wrists when he awoke half way through my tying him up. I understand people do that nowadays for what they think of as fun, for sheer pleasure. *(Short pause.)* Hubby might have gotten away, but I had my revolver at the ready and managed to secure him the rest of the way, a good sturdy cast iron bed too. Your father quite by accident happened upon this little scene of mine. Hubby and I lived two doors up the street and Jacob had stopped by for I'm not sure what, and there we were. He called his secretary and took the day off, your mother never knew about it, and your father never spoke of it again. He tried to negotiate an agreement between hubby and me, 'till he was blue in the face. That was his skill, his calling. How he talked and talked at me, 'till my ears simply buzzed. He drank glasses and glasses of water. He peed in the hallway water closet with the door open and still he kept us all talking. At sundown I relented, a very long day, thirty-six hours. I let hubby disappear off into whatever woods his wounded bull self found. Jacob went home leaving me alone, having covered me with a blanket on the sofa. The next morning I awoke, realized all that had happened the day before. There were the severed sash cords showing evidence of something other than a dream. I felt suffocated for air, and tried to open the windows. I thought I would certainly choke to death. I became so annoyed with the un-weighted unco-operative windows that I found I had to shoot them out with the smallest of shotguns, a little squirrel hunting rifle, just to get the air moving. And given the thirty-six hours I'd been through, and the fact that I still couldn't breathe, I helped myself to the rarest of treats and had a tiny suckle on the nipple of a poppy, so to speak. I was untying a rubber medical elastic from my biceps and putting away the stainless syringe when a neighbour, no doubt curious about the shooting came in. My, was she scandalized. I sat there on the cold terra cotta kitchen floor smiling, as warm as a wood stove. A pleasant heat guttering inside me, like the flame on a hardwood log, three-quarters spent. *(Pause.)* It was shortly after that I was asked by a *number* of the neighbours, one evening on my porch, to find somewhere else to live. Can you imagine the nerve? *So* in those dainty thirty-six hours, I had occasion to need the scotch, the gun and the opium. And Auntie always tells the truth.

ANNE   You make my mouth hurt with smiling, as I listen to you.

BEA   And doesn't God just love to look at you smiling? There's *radiance* in your smile.

ANNE   I think you'll make me cry.

BEA   Go ahead, dear. *(Pause.)* You can't hold back tears, or laughter, or gas. You get cancer.

ANNE   *(Sobbing loudly.)* Thanks-a-lot..

BEA   ..I didn't mean it. Well, yes I did. It's completely true.

ANNE   *(Sobbing louder.)* No.

BEA   STOP IT. Even a good thing can be overdone.

ANNE   All right.. *(Blowing her nose.)* All right.

BEA   There all done and better.

ANNE   Tell me Auntie, that I didn't kill Bill.

BEA   You know perfectly well that you did. You
            wore him down to a mere nub of a man, and he
            died from exhaustion as much as anything.

ANNE   *(Crying again.)* No Auntie, no I didn't.

BEA   OF COURSE YOU DIDN'T. It was God's will or
            something.. totally inescapable and meaningful
            like that.. something somehow right and.. ugly
            and beautiful all at the same time..

ANNE   Do you believe that?

BEA   Don't push me. I'm trying to be golden and
            nice.

ANNE   Did you mean it? That God loves to look at me.

BEA   Yes, even when you make a trumpet sound
            blowing your nose.

ANNE   Thank you, Auntie. What does it mean?

BEA   It means.. you're entertainment for God.

ANNE   Like a joke, some kind of cosmic joke?

BEA   No. Like company. Like someone to keep God
            company.

ANNE   That's a nice thought.

BEA   *(Pause.)* Miserable thoughts are a penny a
            dozen; nice thoughts you usually pay for, dear-
            ly dear. Hold onto it, it's yours for free. Now, if
            you are going to shoot a moose.

ANNE   If I what?

BEA   If you are going to shoot a moose with a hand-gun...

ANNE   Yes?

BEA   Later. I'll tell you later, dear.

ACT TWO
Scene Two

Seven screens house left, three screens house right. As the lights come up, ANNE is typing in a steady, rhythmic way. She is counting to herself under her breath. BETH is now seven months pregnant.

BETH   I thought you'd like some company.

ANN   I have company. I am company.

BETH   Someone to talk to. Someone real.

ANNE   Send them away, whoever it is, send them away.

BETH   She's a nice lady, older than you but very...

ANNE   You beg me to write, then you interrupt, and interrupt...

BETH   I'd like it, ideally, if you wrote something more than.. simple numbers.

ANNE   Numbers are beautiful. They also happen to be perfect, and are beyond all criticism. Five, six and seven. As elegant, as heaven. And now a surprise, some surprise numbers, a real shocker, ready? *(Bracing herself.)* Eight, nine and... *(Pause. Disappointed with herself.)* Rips your skirt off doesn't it?

BETH   ..No. I'm going to bring her in.

ANNE   What for?

BETH   I thought you might like a visitor.

ANNE   I'd rather have.. a

BETH   ..What?

ANNE   I'm thinking. A..

BETH   No witticism. So, you get a visitor.

ANNE   I'm not having a...

BETH   We'll just see how it works.

ANNE   Who's going to work on my book if someone's in here?

BETH   Just meet her..

ANNE   ...Will you write the numbers for me for a while, just seven eight and nine, nothing else. *(Short pause.)* You can use zeros but no ones.

BETH   If you need me to.. yes.

ANNE   This is what's keeping things on an even keel for me, for the moment. This nice steady repetition of numbers. I don't want it interrupted, it'd make me berserk.

BETH   Okay, I'd be happy to share the typing.

ANNE   You can't just type, you have to write.. invent the numbers fresh all over, contemplate them.

BETH   I'll do my best.

> *PAULA STERN enters. [It is the same actress that plays BEA. She needs to differentiate the character somewhat. She should have a different costume, perhaps a simple robe. PAULA could have a slight German or Eastern European accent. as long as the character does not become caricature.*

BETH   Anne Hirsch, Paula Stern..

ANNE   *(To BETH.)* Get writing.

                BETH exits, but we still see her in the
                background throughout the scene.

PAULA   I'm told you haven't been well.

ANNE   .. I'm told I'm clinically... that I'm insane.

PAULA   So we have something in common, we've both
           been told something about you. *(Pause.)* I was
           once told I was clinically something, now I'm
           okay. What's that mean anyway? You're in a
           clinic, they tell you you're clinical...

ANNE   *(Turning around.)* You're my Aunt Bea..

PAULA   What?

ANNE   You are my Aunt Bea.. It's as plain as your face.
           Don't deny it.

PAULA   Well now..

ANNE   Don't be mean, Aunt Bea.

PAULA   Listen it's possible, maybe, I look like your
           Aunt.

ANNE   You are.

PAULA   I remind you of her. Stranger things have hap-
           pened under God's bright heavens, blessed be..
           (She tenderly touches ANNE's cheek, with the back
           of her hand.)

ANNE   You're touching me.

PAULA   So that you'll see me. Really see me. Look close,
           who is it that I am?

ANNE   ..Oh.

PAULA   Do you see me?

ANNE   ..Yes.

PAULA   ..So it's possible you were mistaken, don't feel bad. It can happen to anyone. There once was a man got his wife's face and a hat all mixed up.

ANNE   There's always something to look forward to.

PAULA   You have a nice hat, very nice. You got it where?

ANNE   Rotman's hat shop—Chinatown.

PAULA   I know Rotman; still alive? Bless him. It's a nice hat. You're lucky.

ANNE   Why do you say I'm lucky?

PAULA   'Cause you've got a nice hat, things could be worse.

ANNE   It's my husband's hat, was his, is his...

PAULA   Luckier still.

ANNE   Why?

PAULA   A husband, yet? So much going for you, what are you doing in here?

ANNE   I'm not sure if he's.. I'm still trying to sort out what's what.

PAULA   A good plan. I'd like you to take one of my cards, okay? In case you should need anything from me.

ANNE   ..Okay.

PAULA   Here, let's get a look. I gotta' whole stack a' cards in one of my pockets, they could be in

this, no, they could be in.. no. Here. Yes. Let's
sit. We're going to read, we should sit, all right?

ANNE Fine.

PAULA And they say you're crazy, feh. *(Pause.)* What
can they ever know?

> *The two women sit down across from each
> other on the bed. After a moment.*

PAULA You're name is Hirsch?

ANNE Yes.

PAULA Your husband's.

ANNE Yes.

PAULA Your father's?

ANNE Aaron.

PAULA Your father's mother: Michaels. Your father the
lawyer son of the Rabbi Aaron, a good lawyer;
your grandfather a gifted Rabbi. His father and
his father and his father, Aaron all the way back
to quite possibly...

ANNE So you're at the far and extreme end of expert-
ise in Jewish geography, I'm impressed. You
grew up with my..?

PAULA I'm a Rabbi. I'm meant to know. Knowing is
meaning. I'm the three hundred and first
female Rabbi in history; that's *known* anyway.
Which brings us back to.. my card. I'd like you
to have a my card.

ANNE Good lord.

PAULA Precisely my thought... Look, pick a card, take
any one of these...

ANNE   Is this a magic trick?

PAULA   Yes. Yes it is Anne Hirsch, by magic, I'm here to see you today. So look at the card..

ANNE   It's blank, both sides.

PAULA   You drew a blank! How interesting. Let me try. Here, mine's got writing on it. And this one, and this one. Must have been an odd card out, you got. This one, writing, this one. Try again, it get's better.

ANNE   *(Selecting more carefully.)* Blank, both sides.

PAULA   Impossible! Two in a row. Here look through them carefully for yourself..

ANNE   *(After she has looked through twenty or so cards.)* All with writing. *(Reading.)* "1-800-Rab-Weds." What's this?

PAULA   A calling card. If people can't find me, how could I be expected to appear before them? That's why I want you to have one. But it has to be the one you choose. I don't think you're just about to get married are you?

ANNE   They're different?

PAULA   Of course, different for everyone. Choose once more.

ANNE   I'm getting annoyed.

PAULA   No, you're not. You say you are, you're not. Choose.

ANNE   *(Takes card.)* BLANK.

PAULA   Nu, three blank cards! So something's up with you, sweets. What could it be?

ANNE   A smart alec Rabbi.

PAULA: ...Yes. A little trickster of a Rabbiness. A goenif, and a yingele. You know what that means?

ANNE   Sure.

PAULA   Tell me, smartycakes.

ANNE   A thief and a gypsy.

PAULA   Right. Good girl. Let me give you a card. *(Displaying the cards, back up.)* Pick one.

ANNE   This is it, after this, I'm tired.

PAULA   No. No, you're not. Pick.

ANNE   "1-800-Rab-Help."

PAULA   If you need help, you call me. *(Pause.)* Don't look sour, I could help.

ANNE   Thank you.

PAULA   I'm also putting one in this hat of yours. Just inside the brim, in the band. You know why?

ANNE   No. Everything's a big mystery with you..

PAULA   Correct. Everything's a big mystery. Everything.

ANNE   Why are you putting it in the band?

PAULA   Now she wants to know. I'll tell you why. *(Pause.)* You're walking down the street, suddenly along comes a wind from out of nowhere. Who's wind? It's a mystery, but it takes from you your hat. The hat blows away on the street. You chase after it, and chase and chase. But still that hat blows away, faster than the wind. The sail that is the hat being carried at the square root of the velocity of the wind,

times the surface area of the hat, times the
angle of incidence to the wind. That's a little
mathematics for the rationalists. The hat flies
away accelerating into infinity and eternity,
only the friction of the air somewhat slowing
its progress toward a sonic boom and eventually it's surpassing the speed of light and then
becoming the great cosmic hat, the original
mathematic code, which is the Heavens and
Earth, that which gives us shelter from rain,
Manna from Heaven, et al.

ANNE   *(A long pause, ANNE is mesmerized. Wiping away
a few tears.)* All right, so it's quite a fast hat..

PAULA   I shouldn't talk?

ANNE   No, please go on.

PAULA   Then be good. Yes. Very fast, and who knows
why? Mathematics? Mystery. Your hat flies into
another neighbourhood altogether. There no
one knows it's the hat of a big fancy writer
lady. It's just a hat. No big mystery. But then
they pick up this hat. What do they find? A little card in the band, on the inside of the brim.
The person is curious. They look at the card.
On the card it says "1-800-Rab-Help". Thinking
it's the hat of a Rabbi, and after all, how far off
are they? It's the hat of the daughter of the son,
of the son of etc. and so on back to Israelites.
They call. I go to their house, I get the hat. I call
you. *(Pause.)* Now *(Short pause.)* you've got the
card, the hat, a Rabbi in your house and conse-
quently a visitor. *(Pause.)* So get me some tea.

ANNE   *(Pause.)* I like that, I like that a lot.

PAULA   That's a *beginning*. Liking something. There's a
foundation. Where's my tea?

ANNE   I don't know.. I don't have any.

PAULA A lady with such a nice hat, no tea? I don't believe it.

ANNE Well I don't.

PAULA Think again.

ANNE More riddles..

PAULA You don't like?

ANNE I like fine, I don't know where..

PAULA You brought your favourite tea cups, where are they?

ANNE *(Thinking hard, then pointing.)* In the top drawer of that dresser.

PAULA So go look. Go now.

> *ANNE walks over to dresser and opens the top drawer. Sparks come flying out of the open drawer.*

PAULA Try the second drawer..

> *ANNE pulls a stainless steel kettle out of the second drawer, which has a steady stream of steam coming out of it.*

PAULA There, you see. So make me some, I'm a guest..

ANNE How do you take it?

PAULA Whatever you've got. *(Pause.)* A little honey, buckwheat honey I like, some fresh lemon. Earl grey is nice. And ginger snaps.

ANNE You think you're in a tea shop?

PAULA I'm in you.. in your home, that is. Is this where you're staying? So look in the drawer.

> *ANNE finds everything that was described and takes it out of the drawer, putting it on top of the dresser.*

ANNE   This is strange..

PAULA   A very tiny trick. A yingele trick.

ANNE   *(Almost to herself.)* She was a lady. A tea society lady. A hurly-burly, hell in your face, boiling pot of water broad.

PAULA   What's that, dearie?

ANNE   Something..

PAULA   Is it?

ANNE   No, it's nothing.

PAULA   It's something, it's nothing. Now *you've* got a mystery.

ANNE   What have you come here for?

PAULA   I was invited. I'm a guest.

ANNE   Who was it that invited you?

PAULA   You did.

ANNE   Beth, Dr. Beth Ottis, no?

PAULA   Beth brought me here. You called upon me. You counted on me by calling my name, you called me by name, by counting..

ANNE   I did?

PAULA   Yes. *(Pause.)* Do you know why people call on me? Why they ask me to marry them, for example?

ANNE   No.

PAULA   Think about it. I'm also a Justice of the Peace,
          by the powers vested in me.. I am the law, I am
          the law, I am the law.

ANNE   I see.

PAULA   Like your father's father, my father was a Rabbi
          and his and his. After years of study, a doctor-
          ate in theology, I thought who am I to break the
          chain?

ANNE   ..I don't know if I asked you here.

PAULA   I know. (*Taking a tefillen strap from her pocket.*)
          You know what this is?

ANNE   A piece of leather, what is this? It looks familiar.

PAULA   It's a piece of tefillen, an entirely different mat-
          ter, form of matter.

ANNE   It's my father's, my father's strap..

PAULA   *My father's.* A coincidence perhaps, they both
          kept a piece of something, the piece that was
          left.

ANNE   ..Not very likely.

PAULA   What could be more alike, and likely? My
          great, great grandfather used this in Poland.
          You've heard of Kabbalah?

ANNE   ..Yes.

PAULA   Everyone in my father's village, in the country
          even, believed he possessed mystical knowl-
          edge beyond normal men, and powers..

ANNE   They did?

PAULA   He would bind them with tefillen, say prayers, their ailments would vanish into thin air, into the wind..

ANNE   I don't believe..

PAULA   Yes you do, you of all people.. I was given what was left of his tefillen, as well as a particular gift of healing.

ANNE   You're getting it all mixed up. This is one of my stories. I was given what was left of my father's tefillen and powers of understanding...

PAULA   I'm not mixed up. I'm very definitely not. I'd like to offer you something. I'd like to say a prayer with you and bind the tefillen to your arm.

ANNE   *(A slight pause.)* ARE YOU OUT OF YOUR MIND? For men, that's a ritual for men, a ritual I performed with my husband when he was not well...

PAULA   Something that happens in more than one time and place is not typically less true, it is all the more true.

ANNE   WHO SAID I NEED HEALING?

PAULA   Where are you, dear?

ANNE   *(Through her teeth.)* A mental health care facility.

PAULA   I rest my argument. Rest yours. I'd like to help. I'm going to place the tefillen on your arm...

ANNE   NO YOU'RE NOT. You're not going to, while I'm still breathing. Where's Beth. Where in God's name is she?

PAULA   Right there. Look, you see her. She's at a distance. That's where you've put her.

ANNE   She's sitting at my typewriter. She's writing.

PAULA   Yes and who do you think she could possibly be? A mental health care worker, a dedicated woman who one day sits down and discovers she has a gift for writing. Who likes it so much, she doesn't hear when people call out her name at the top of their lungs?

ANNE   ..She looks a little like me.

PAULA   A version of you. You in another time and place, as another person. You some time away.

ANNE   Get her back here, she talks a scientific babble, which is insulting, even upsetting, but there's something...

PAULA   She tried. She'll be back, you'll bring her back with your mind.

ANNE   I want you gone.

PAULA   Careful what you wish for..

ANNE   I do.

PAULA   That's twice you've said it.

ANNE   Better, I want you to admit that you're my Aunt Bea.

PAULA   You have to be careful, the things you call upon, what you ask for, wish for and want. They will come. To you in particular, and especially now.

ANNE   I wish you would admit you are my Aunt Bea.

PAULA   What possible good could that do us?

ANNE   I could prove to the Doctor that I'm not crazy. I could go home.

PAULA   And I'd be locked up again. Please, try to think
        rationally. Let me bind your arm with the phy-
        lactery.

                    There is a moment of silence. PAULA
                    begins to bind ANNE's arm. ANNE is
                    still.

ANNE   *(Suddenly yelling.)* AAAahhh. Aunt Bea. I wish
        it, I wish it, I wish it.

PAULA   Now you've done it. What is this? I drive all the
        way from as far as there is; I talk to you non-
        stop. *(She gets twenty-six ounces of scotch out the*
        top drawer, pours herself a big drink. The actress
        changes her costume, by taking off a robe. Speaking
        as BEA.) I try to make sense of what you're say-
        ing... Tell you that you'll be all right..

ANNE   *(Short pause.)* It is you.

BEA   If you are going to shoot a moose with a hand-
        gun... you had better be very, very close. A full
        grown moose can weigh as much as an old
        fashioned Chevrolet; you don't want that kind
        of weight even dimly aware of the fact that you
        have just tried, half heartedly, to kill it. There
        are times dearie, when you may have to kill a
        moose and that is all there is to it. Whether or
        not it's in season will not matter in such a case.
        A woman may occasionally need to kill a
        moose to feed herself and her family. Years and
        years ago, out west, the Second World War was
        winding to a close and there was very little for
        a lady or her family to eat. I was taking care of
        your grandparents at the time, and contrary to
        popular belief old people do need to eat some-
        thing now and again.. I was doing the dishes
        over a steaming hot sink full of water, looking
        out over the vegetable garden that we kept out-
        side the kitchen window so it could be
        watched, when a bull moose appeared slowly,
        standing in the lettuce patch. He moved so qui-

etly, so steadily I thought it was your gran'
moving an old hide of some sort along the
clothesline for airing. He came fully into view, a
magnificent male. He rolled his head just a little
at the top of his neck and then began to eat all
our lettuce. Not some of it, all of it. I grabbed
my forty-five from the sideboard thinking I'd
fire a shot to scare him off. When I saw him
though, once I was in the garden–all I could
think of was meat. Have you ever had a moose
steak with wild mushrooms, and boiled bull
rush root? It's a close second to a good night
of.. whatever you like best, dear. There he was
eating all of my lettuce, a half summer's worth.
I went back into the kitchen, quietly as I could,
slipped my dress off to tell you the truth, so the
noise of it wouldn't twig him. A finished cotton
day dress that was noisy like wax paper. Also
moose blood is thick as molasses and stains
badly. I put some sugar in my hand.. I walked
around the house and approached him quietly,
no shoes.. There I was, bra and panties, forty-
five-calibre-revolver—damn fine solidly crafted
gun—stalking this moose from down wind,
hoping like hell to eat him. I got within a foot
of him before he fully noticed me. I think I was
tip toeing on hunger, riding a fairy of mouth-
watering desire. There are three and only three
ways that I know of to kill a moose, actually
kill, not maim, kill. First and best is a clean shot
through the head, bear in mind a bullet or two
have been known to bounce off the forehead of
the creature. Second and not quite as reliable is
if you can open the carotid artery—which probably makes for the best meat as the adrenaline
and hormones don't get a chance to dance in
the bloodstream. Third and far too dicey for a
half-naked lady with a handgun in her garden
is through the poor beast's heart of hearts,
which is hellishly hard to find and could take a
whole magazine of shooting. *(She takes a big
breath and exhales on.)* Whoo, I'm getting hungry,
just talking about the old fella. So I'm a foot off

his rear right quarters, maybe a yard, maybe a foot. I see then, his front leg is all tangled in a piece of rope netting we used to keep animals from the garden. I don't know if he could run or not. He turns around to look at me and could kill me with a half gesture, without even wanting to. Behind my back in my right hand is the revolver, safety off. In my left hand I've got the biggest handful of brown sugar the kitchen could spare, wet with sweat, almost boiling in the palm of my hand. I hold it out, and the sweat is running down my sides in a tickle all the way to my bloomers and damn it I'm silently crying now cause I know I could die, but he's much more likely to. He sniffs and sniffs and licks at the sugar, once twice and it's going into his blood stream and this hungry moose is in moose marsh heaven and doesn't even notice the dull grey gun come up to his forehead. If the gun had jammed as they sometimes can, I don't know what would have happened. One bullet, clean through the head and then the only sound was a sigh as the old mountain went down in the lettuce patch. *(Pause.)* My how we ate. A year or more the three of us. Roasts, steaks, stews, sausages.. Every single sinew of that moose got used, every little bit got used again and again 'cause that's the only way with a moose, you kill yourself.

ANNE Auntie, I feel sick. I think I'm going to need the...

BEA Is it the medication?

ANNE No. It's the story.

   BETH enters, PAULA does not look quite right to her.

BETH Paula, are you all right?

BEA   Paula?

BETH   ...Your name?

BEA   My name is Beatrice Wade.

BETH   Jesus, sweet Jesus, could everybody please stop BEING SO CRAZY so I can get on with my life. *(Pause.)* Your name is Paula Stern.

BEA   *(Bringing out a cannon of a voice.)* DON'T FUCK WITH ME, SWEETIE. I've just driven across the entire continent, half cut. I damn well know who I am. I might not like it all the time, but I know it just the same.

BETH   *(Looking at ANNE.)* What have you done to her? A whole year she's been well, and very strong. When she came to me she was cooking frozen foods in their boxes till they burnt; she was jamming the icemaker on her fridge till her kitchen had a proverbial flood. She tried to light a bucket of water on fire for three hours one day, in a lecture hall with a hundred students in it. A year she's been back at work, a professor and a Rabbi and you've unravelled her completely in half an hour.

        ANNE through the above speech sits on her bed holding onto her package of cigarettes. She is rocking herself back and forth, not listening to the other women. She's speaking to herself under her breath. She strokes the cigarettes as though stroking a forehead.

BEA   *(Overlapping BETH's last sentence.)* Okay, so I consumed the Rabbi lady. Nice old broad, little airy-fairy, little caught in the clouds. Might even be hanging onto a pinch of delusional self-deification, which doesn't say much for your work. You could be next if you don't stop farting around, and make this niece of mine a fully functional non nut-job again, huh?

BETH   Anne

ANNE: I can't, I simply can't. I CAN'T, I CAN'T, I CAN'T. *(ANNE continues to repeat "I can't" quietly four more times.)*

> *N.B. The following noted lines of BILL's are spoken by BEA & BETH together, and not by BILL.*

BILL   *(B&B)* You will...

ANNE   No.

BILL   *(B&B)* Yes you will, you will help me with this.

ANNE   It's not something I can do...

BILL   *(B&B)* I haven't asked for much have I?

ANNE   No, no you haven't.

BILL   *(B&B)* So do this. You owe me.

ANNE   I owe you?

ACT TWO
Scene Three

Eight screens house left, two screens house right. The bed rotates, as it does so, BILL gets into it. Either as a projection, or as a simple mechanical device, there is something representative of a machine for suctioning fluid from BILL's lungs. It should seem to be powered by an orange electrical cord, plugged into a socket. BILL has a clear plastic tube taped in one nostril. BETH and BEA retreat to the very edges of the scene and light.

Dialogue continuous.

BILL You do. Enough to help me with something I can't do alone. The one and only thing I've ever needed your help with. Or ever asked..

ANNE You make it sound like I've never helped..

BILL I've never needed... not like this..

ANNE Not yet Bill.

BILL Then help me to pray for what's best.

ANNE Yes, I will do that.

BILL Wrap my hand with your Father's tefillen...

ANNE All right.

BILL You're comforting me.

ANNE I want to..

BILL ...Do what I ask of you then.

ANNE   ..I'll pray.

BILL   Wrap my hand and forearm seven times.

ANNE   I am.

BILL   Wrap it in such a way...

ANNE   Every time, you still tell me how..

BILL   *(His anger rising.)* Yes, because I TELL YOU. It's my prayer, I tell you how...

ANNE   I don't mind.

BILL   *(A threat.)* I'd do it myself if I could...

ANNE   Stop.

BILL   *(Pause.)* I'd love to.

ANNE   This isn't prayer.

BILL   It is. It's my most devout prayer. Get me my hat please..

ANNE   Yes, all right.

> *ANNE moves towards where his hat, a fedora, is hanging on a hook. BILL unwraps the tefillen from around his hand and forearm and wraps the orange electrical extension cord around the middle finger of his left hand, then around his hand. As this is happening ANNE turns her back to get the hat. She turns back to BILL, hat in hand, and sees what he's done with the power cord. There is a moment of silence between them.*

ANNE   Bill...

BILL   ..You're starting to slip.

ANNE   *(Slight overlapping through 'til both characters speak together.)* Am I?

BILL   Slip.

ANNE   Am..?

BILL   Yes.

ANNE   To..?

BILL   You're slipping into the shimmering mirror of memory..

ANNE   Where..?

BILL   You're falling away from me even as I speak..

ANNE   To..?

BILL   Into the abyss of Time.

ANNE   Into..?

BILL   Into the World of When.

ANNE   Where am I?

BILL   "When."

ANNE   *(Pause.)* ...Oh. *(Pause.)* Oh, I am?

BILL   Who, who tells you what's real?

ANNE   You do.

BILL   Who knows what's real? Who's always known?

ANNE   You. You've always been the one.

BILL   I am. I am the one.

ANNE   You are.

BILL   I'm already gone.. I'm dead but I'm still breathing, breathing badly, a very bad chore..

ANNE   No, don't say that.

BILL   Look at me. Look at me in both eyes, both of your eyes.

ANNE   Bill..

BILL   Do you see the truth?

ANNE   Yes.

BILL   Who knows it?

ANNE   You and I both.

BILL & ANNE   You and I both.

BILL   Tie this tefillen around my arm.

ANNE   It's not a...

BILL   I'm drowning a second at a time for weeks and months and years...

ANNE   *(Hissing.)* I CAN'T HEAR ABOUT THAT.

BILL   *(Hissing back.)* SELFISH.

ANNE   No.

BILL   Who knows?

ANNE   We do, you do, I do.

BILL   Who else?

ANNE   No one.

BILL   No one will. It's only ours. It's the only thing that is only ours.

ANNE   Yes, Bill.

BILL   So no one else *can* know ever, and that is all.

ANNE   Yes Bill.

BILL   Tie the tefillen around my arm.

ANNE   It's an electrical cord.. An orange electrical cord..

BILL   Bind the phylactery to my arm.

ANNE   ...Can't.

BILL   You must, must, you will.

ANNE   Will. *(Pause.)* It's a packet of cigarettes..

BILL   It's a phylactery box with four scrolls inside. Bind it with your father's tefillen strap.

ANNE   Am..

BILL   Wrap it seven times. *(She does, there is still slack in the cord.)*

ANNE   Done.

BILL   No, not done, not yet.

ANNE   Why?

BILL   Three more times, one for each of the Ten Sefirot.

ANNE   Three more.

BILL   Tell me about the Sefirot.

>   (*ANNE unwraps the cord to his wrist.*)

ANNE   There are ten.

BILL   What are they?

ANNE   You know.

BILL   Please, tell me...

ANNE   Beyond the seven levels of heaven; they are the
           God-head. The quintessence of existence;
           everything and nothing. It is the un-speakable,
           the un-seen and the un-known. They are the
           mitzvot, the commandments, the fragments
           from which good must come. They are the fin-
           gers and thumbs on your hands, the organs of
           your body.

BILL   Name them, tell me their names and what they
           mean to us.

ANNE   Shekhinah, Conception. Yesod, Beginning and
           End. Hod, Radiance. Netzah, Infinity. Tipheret,
           Compassion. Gevurah, Judgement. Hesed,
           Grace. Binah, Intelligence. Hokhmah, Wisdom.
           And Keter which is Ayin.

>   As *ANNE says this, she wraps the cord ten
>   times from the wrist up his arm. There is
>   now very little slack left in the cord.*

BILL   Ayin is?

ANNE   Nothingness.

BILL   Say a prayer with me.

ANNE   Bill...

BILL   Annie, you're my Titan, you're my Rabbi, now.
           You're my merciful God. You're my brave girl
           who won't tell a soul.

ANNE   ..I won't?

BILL   You must promise.

ANNE   I do.

BILL   That's it. I do. *(Pause.)* Again.

ANNE   I do.

BILL   Say a prayer with me.. *(ANNE says the following prayer with BILL, BILL leads.)* I will be betrothed to you, forever and always. I will be betrothed to you, without sin, dwelling in Truth, Grace and Compassion. I will be betrothed to you with fidelity, through infinity, and unto HASHEM. Now we are more married than any two people can ever be. Together in purpose, together in Life, together in my Death, and together in Love.

ANNE   ...I will love you for Centuries to Come. *(ANNE leads this prayer and BILL follows.)* I will love you for Centuries to Come. I am my lover's and my lover is mine. I am my lover's and my lover is mine. Anni l'dodi v'dodi li. Anni l'dodi v'dodi li. Anni l'dodi v'dodi li.

> *BILL suddenly jerks his arm hard. His motion pulls the plug right out of the socket, as it is intended to. The motion of the lung suction machine stops. ANNE sees this and sees that it is BILL's intention. There is a long moment of silence. ANNE and BILL simply look at one another. BILL coughs a little at first then quickly this turns to a convulsive and violent action. He is drowning in his own fluid. There is a moment's calm.*

BILL   Help me.

> *ANNE moves, somewhat in shock, towards the plug to re-start the machine. BILL's movements and sounds let her know this is not what he means. ANNE stands behind BILL and strokes his forehead as he begins another fit of coughing; he looks as though he's in terrible pain. He is making sounds.*

BILL   Hel.. He.. p.. H–lp.

> *ANNE slowly places a pillow over his face, leaving BILL the opportunity to stop her. She presses down on the pillow with her full force as his body convulses.*

ANNE   Anni l'dodi v'dodi li. Anni l'dodi v'dodi li. Anni l'dodi v'dodi li. I will love you for Centuries to Come. Centuries to Come. Centuries.

> *BILL's body gives out and he dies relatively quietly under ANNE's prayer. ANNE sits on the bed, takes the pillow off BILL's face. She hyperventilates, then her breath moves to sobs and heaving. Her body shudders from top to bottom. She gets off the bed and walks away from it a small distance. There is a long silence where ANNE stands simple and still. She moves back to the chair beside the bed, and addresses BILL.*

ANNE   *(Very quietly.)* I will be fine.

ACT TWO
Scene Four

Nine screens house left, one screen house right. We are in the hospital room again. BETH OTTIS is no longer pregnant, she has given birth.

ANNE   I've told you everything there is.

BETH   Yes.

ANNE   Now I want to go home.

BETH   That's a lovely idea, I'd like to see that happen too.

ANNE   So what's preventing it?

BETH   You tell me, what's in the way.

ANNE   You'd like to know that I can tell the difference between an infant, my deceased husband and a packet of cigarettes..

BETH   Yes. That would be helpful don't you think?

ANNE   ..I know the difference.

BETH   Not always you don't. A lot depends on how you do today. On this particular interview. You'll be assessed. *(She turns on a cassette recorder.)* I'm going to record it, is that okay?

ANNE   Yes. *(Pause.)* How is your daughter?

BETH   She's good. She smiles. *(Short pause.)* Let's start with the very basics, shall we?

The actress we saw first as BEA and later as PAULA appears just beside BETH. Her

> *costume is almost identical to BETH's. She*
> *now has something of BETH's manner.*

BEA *(as BETH)* Let's start with the very basics, shall we?

ANNE *(Looking at her a long moment.)* Yes.

BETH Who am I?

ANNE *(With a little laugh.)* We're starting very simply, aren't we..?

BEA *(as BETH)* Please, answer..

> *ANNE speaks mostly to BETH, as though*
> *she thinks BEA as BETH is an imagining.*

ANNE You are my long-time psychiatrist.

BETH Good. *(Pause.)* My name?

ANNE Beth, Dr. Beth Ottis. I get a point?

BEA *(as BETH)* It's not a point game. It's a little more global. *(Pause.)* Who is Bill Hirsch?

ANNE Bill *was* my husband, he died two years ago. He died from inoperable lung cancer.

BETH Good.

ANNE It didn't seem very good to me at the time..

BETH The answer, the answer was good.

ANNE Was it right?

BEA *(as BETH)* You tell me?

ANNE Yes, it's the right and only answer. *(To herself.)* When does a candle stop burning? When it stops.

BETH   Are you responsible for Bill's death?

ANNE   Not directly, no, no I'm not. He died of natural causes.

BEA   *(as BETH)* Who is Beatrice Wade?

ANNE   Beatrice Wade was, and is, my mother's sister.

BEA   *(as BETH)* Where is she now?

ANNE   No one really knows, she disappeared.

BEA   *(as BETH)* Has she been here to see you?

ANNE   Not exactly..

BEA   *(as BETH)* And you mean by that..?

ANNE   She's here now. She's here in you and me...

BEA   *(as BETH)* Anne, think carefully. Am I Beatrice Wade?

ANNE looks at BETH.

ANNE   No. Dr. Beth Ottis.

BETH   So, is she here?

ANNE   In my imagination...

BEA   *(as BETH)* But where is she really?

ANNE   No one knows.

BETH   So far, you are doing very well. *(Pause.)* What would you do if you were not allowed to go home today?

ANNE   *(She gets out of her chair walks a distance to one side, she speaks to herself.)* I would consume you. I would eat you down into a steely stomach

even if you scratched my gizzard out on the
way. I would be, while you're in mine, in your
stomach and would swell up your liver 'till it
popped and poisoned your blood, running
rivers of ulcers through you.

BETH   Anne, I'm waiting..

ANNE   Didn't I answer?

BEA   *(as BETH)* No. You said nothing.

ANNE   I must have spoken to myself.

BETH   What will you do if you can't go home..?

ANNE   *(She smiles.)* I will wait patiently, the patient
patient, 'till I am ready.

BETH   I think you may well go home. I want you to
concentrate however as it will help. What will
you do when you go home?

ANNE   I will continue with my work. I will take meas-
ured steps when walking.

BEA   *(as BETH)* What does that mean?

ANNE   I will hold onto the sometimes thin edge of
reality as best I can. Steadily, I will.

BETH   And your work, what do you plan?

ANNE   I have begun a book based losely on the character of my Aunt Bea. That will be first. A book
about a woman, who becomes so eccentric that
she eventually disappears altogether.

BEA   *(as BETH)* Fine. After that.

ANNE   I'm thinking of a book about a woman that
goes through a spiritual awakening, a professor
of theology who comes to realize she is a Rabbi.

BEA   *(as BETH)* And these will be stories of real people?

ANNE   Based losely on my impressions of people, as I have encountered them. Fictionalized beyond all recognition.

BEA   *(as BETH)*After that?

ANNE   I've started another book about a woman losely based on myself. I can't honestly say which of these will be finished first.

BETH   How much writing have you done towards these novels? These are novels?

ANNE   Yes. The one based on my Aunt, a hundred and fifty pages, thoroughly fictionalized. She might or might not recognize herself.

BEA   *(as BETH)* Were she to see it..?

ANNE   Yes. Also heavily fictionalized, the story of the Rabbi, right now I have seventy pages.

BETH   And the last, the one based on yourself?

ANNE   Less pages, thirty or so.

BEA   *(as BETH)* This is good, you've done well.

ANNE   Thank you.

BETH   I still have a few questions, if that's alright.

ANNE   Go on. I have a few myself.

BEA   *(as BETH to ANNE.)* What did you want to ask?

ANNE   How is it that I became well?

BETH   It's complex.

ANNE   Tell me about it..

BEA   *(as BETH)* You are just beginning to be well again. I will have to see you once a week at a minimum, twice weekly to begin with.

ANNE   That's fine, tell me, how did I..?

BETH   The disease which is, *was* pervasive, delusional, biochemically a reality nonetheless...

ANNE   A LITTLE more simply please.

BEA   *(as BETH)* The brain chemistry changes gradually, even without drugs.

ANNE   Changes and then?

BEA   *(As BETH)* It is a gradual process, a letting go. How does anyone kick the habit of suffering? Heroin, alcohol, self-inflicted misery of any kind? They're all heads of the same Medusa. In your case, the monster died from the absurdity which constructed it. The imagination could no longer support it.

ANNE   ..And the disease has the resilience of a shark on a fishing line?

BETH   Yes. And may escape, the disease may live on, it must always be watched. Partly though, it is the disease of being alive.

ANNE   What else did you want to ask of me?

BETH turns to the cassette recorder off.

BEA *(as BETH)*
& BETH Does it still seem real to you? The idea of your aunt visiting etc.

ANNE   It *seems* very real. I know it's not. *(BEA disappears.)* And yet, it is perhaps more real than what is said to be real. Could I, for example, be your Aunt? Let me tell you what I know of it. Are there parts of you that are similar to parts of me? Yes. Can one person ever truly be another? No, of course not. Can one be dead and alive at the same time? They came to visit in my mind, as they always have. Am I my Aunt Bea? In some small way, yes. Though not as I see her, more as I might be. In the imagination anything is possible. In the real life-span of the Universe, in the billions upon billions of years that have passed, with humankind a match's scratching flare in that history.. The briefest of sparks in an endless winter of long black blue nights... What of that which is beyond this Universe? "We are as a grain of sand on the circumference of the moon. The moon is a grain of sand on the circumference of our Universe. Our Universe is a grain of sand upon the *immeasurable* circumference of Ayin." I'm paraphrasing like mad from mystical writing–research for the Rabbi book. What's real? I sit here, my name is Anne Hirsch. You sit across from me, my long-time doctor. Your name is Beth Ottis. I have lived in my aunt, as she has lived in me, as I did in my mother, as I did even in my husband. *(Pause.)* As I do at times in you and you in me.

(BETH and ANNE laugh at this final rich proposition.)

BETH   It's just fine, you will be fine.

ACT TWO
Scene Five

Ten screens house left. We see on the
screens that we are at a bookstore, inside. A
voice announces: "Ladies and Gentlemen,
ANNE Hirsch."

ANNE   I am pleased to be here. I am pleased to see you
all. *(She opens a book and reads.)* A few too many
people had slipped from Hannah Rosenblum's
life. Slipped through her fingers, fallen from
her bed, and home, and family, into the deep
aching earthy crack of time. She had noticed at
first, she had mourned.. but it had not stopped
the procession of those who seemed, always, to
be leaving her. Hannah in those years seemed
at times a caricature to herself. Lionized by
some, practically prayed to by others in front of
classrooms, thought privately to be a terrible
bitch and a crank, a recluse, a great catch as a
dinner guest—a reliably obtuse and deliberate-
ly volatile old bird. She had come through the
years to live with her own cannibalistically
inclined "anecdotalitis", her necrotizing imagin-
ings. To one, to one in particular, she was a
very special and taxing Titan. To another, perhaps herself, she was still at times the small girl
that everyone jokingly called: "Bea's Niece."

End.

AFTERWORD

The following scene or story originally ended the play. It played continuously from where the play now ends. It is not strictly necessary and risks belabouring the ending. For interest sake it is included. It could be included in the program in place of author's notes.

Permission to include it in playing must be obtained from the author.

BEA appears.

BEA & ANNE together
"HANDLE ROUGH. CONTENTS BROKEN. THIRD- CLASS-SURFACE-MAIL."

ANNE   It was a most peculiar package, which had arrived for Hannah's seventh birthday. The mailman had proven himself possessed of a wild and varied vocabulary cursing the thing, as he hauled it stubbornly from his truck to the doorstep. "Quite a lot of swearing." Hannah had remarked to him, from half behind a bush, causing him to twist his neck in a way he never really forgot. "It weighs more than you could possibly imagine," he offered as an explanation, holding the back of his neck, as though his head might come off otherwise. *(Pause.)* Hannah's dad, Jacob, put the thing in the kitchen. It was "...almost as big as a breadbox," he said through grinding teeth, barely getting his fingers out from under it, as it banged onto the table's soft maple top, leaving a forever mark. Wrapped in brown paper, that seemed scorched by fire, the package looked as though it had been around the world twice. A quarter covered with stamps. It was, of course, from Hannah's Aunt Bea. Even before the birthday cake, even before her absolute favourite dinner, it had to be opened. With the paper off, folded,

put away for some unspecified "later," the black
cast iron box looked menacing. It looked to
have once been a part of a woodstove, but
exactly what part? The screws undone, the
wooden top taken off, an oily-old-rag covered
something... "Be prepared..." said Evelyn, warn-
ing her daughter, and wondering not quite
aloud "..what in hell?" *(Pause.)* "Ta da." said
Hannah pulling away the rag. Here was curios-
ity itself. The entire black box was filled with
glass and coins. Slowly the pieces of something
became apparent to the mystified trio: mother,
father, daughter. Daughter fished out and read
a note:

BEA   "Here's a big glass piggy bank, for little
Hannah, on her seventh. Broken before
shipped–do not be disappointed. The coins are
yours, dearie, if you can get them out without
covering or cutting your hands, or taking the
currency out with any other thing."

ANNE   Hannah was amazed. "Wow!" And they were
there; pig's ears, and feet and belly and snout
all broken up evenly and thoroughly mixed
with silver and nickel and copper pieces.
(Pause.) Evelyn almost cried and Jacob couldn't
help chuckling. The mood of the birthday cele-
bration was at least altered. "What on earth is
she thinking..? A seven year old!" Hannah
heard her mother half-shriek, listening from the
top of the stairs holding the newel post, long
after she'd been put to bed. Hannah loved it.
"It's the BEST present ever." she told herself
about twenty-one times before falling asleep.
(Pause.) She loved the riddle. It took her two
days to figure out what to do and two whole
years to execute her plan. She thought of water
and magnets, strainers, and filters... rolling it
down a hill, filling it with mercury... it was simply the best puzzle anywhere. Finally Hannah
put the black box on the back porch and filled
it part way with sand. Everyday for two years,

almost everyday, she turned the sand, the glass and the coins—there always seemed to be more coins—with a broken handled, small size garden spade. Jacob and Evelyn knew about it, but after a month or two it seemed normal, like a fish tank or something. A hobby. *(Pause.)* On the day of her ninth birthday Hannah was able to fish through the box-barehanded, cutting herself not at all, the glass' edges quite worn out by sand, time and the incredible persistence of a small child. The coins were recognizable, barely, but still... Hannah got Jacob to bring the box to the kitchen table, place it in its forever mark. He sat down and flipped through his prayer book, his Siddur. Before the cake, before dinner, Hannah placed the coins now wrapped in paper rollers beside the black vault, now filled with sand and smooth fragments of piggy bank glass. She asked her mother for the brown paper cover, put it back on the package... tied it up good with heavy string. Hannah asked Evelyn for an indelible marker. She began writing on the package. "CONTENTS UN-BREAK-ABLE." "HANDLE AS YOU PLEASE." "THIRD-CLASS-SURFACE-MAIL." *(As ANNE is finishing this phrase, BEA gets up and exits laughing.)* "What are you doing now, child?" asked Evelyn. "Mailing it back to Aunt Bea," was the response. *(Pause, she puts down her reading.)* If you like the story go buy the book.